CROSS ROADS

Has America made too many wrong turns to find its way home?

James Downey

Cross Roads

Cross Roads

CROSS ROADS
By James Downey
Copyright © 2023

All rights reserved. No part of this book may be reproduced, stored in a retrieval system, or transmitted in any form by any means—electronic, mechanical, photocopy, recording, scanning, or other—except for brief quotations in critical reviews or articles without the written permission of the author.

Unless otherwise noted, Scripture texts and any references to marginal comments used in this work are derived from The NIV Quest Study Bible published by Zondervan, Grand Rapids MI 49546, © 1994, 2003, 2011, by Zondervan; NEW INTERNATIONAL VERSION ®. NIV ® are registered trademarks of Biblica, Inc. ®. Used by permission of Zondervan. All rights reserved worldwide.

ISBN: 978-1-950105-54-0

Line Editor: Patrick Fogarty
Cover Design: Lewis Agrell

Granite Publishing
Prescott-Dublin-Dover

Dedication

To our dear children and grandchildren, and for those who recognize the peril of a misguided trajectory. Learn from the past, and find the truth that will set you and your country free.

Acknowledgments

America's trajectory since 2020 has awakened many to the reality that our circumstances have rapidly deteriorated. The causes have been thoroughly dissected within a study group I was recently invited to join, most of whom are military veterans. As our combined ages exceed 500 years, it is safe to say that we have "real-time" experience with a significant portion of U.S. history.

It became clear in our discussions that there is a vacuum of knowledge amongst many in our country concerning our history and particularly our founding principles. Our desire to preserve and pass that on, as well as how our departure from those principles has precipitated our national downfall, became the catalysts for *Cross Roads*.

My thanks and appreciation to Bill Hunter, Roger Hall, Jim O'Leary, Bill King, Dave Broadwater, and Ernest Ramirez for their service and for their insights, observations, and encouragement to move forward with this effort. We hope that the country we love and served can recover its bearings and once again become a light to the rest of the world.

Preface

An upcoming trip to Ireland mandated a thorough study of driving and navigating its roads. I had heard that motoring there is not for the faint-hearted. Various maps were recommended. Some sources were adamant that an Ireland-specific GPS is essential. After distilling the information gathered, I ordered the most-recommended road atlas. I also got a GPS with our rental car. As we made our way through the country, we found that both were needed to avoid becoming hopelessly lost. The driving tips prepared us for some nerve-wracking encounters on the narrow country roads with tour buses and trucks. If we had made that trip assuming we could just "wing it" without the sound advice gleaned from the experiences of others, our vacation could have been miserable.

We understand the value of learning to navigate through unfamiliar and challenging locales from those who have made the journey before us. Curiously, we seem to assume we can navigate life and steer our country in the right direction relying upon our own wits and often-false assumptions without considering the wisdom and hard lessons learned by our forebears.

Ample advice abounds on how and where to direct our lives as well as our country to avoid their undoing. When we fail to follow that guidance, we end up asking the question that permeates our conversation in 2023: "How did America come to this?"

Our decline has not occurred "overnight," nor by accident. We were warned how to avoid this at the time of our founding, and more significantly by events that occurred thousands of years ago.

Cross Roads chronicles segments of both world and American history, highlighting people, events, and ideologies that have contributed to America's decline. In addition to the human components, *Cross Roads* explores a subject we tend to shun with our Western materialist/scientific mind set: do influences from a spiritual dimension affect our physical world and our lives? If you are skeptical about this, or the existence of God, I once shared the same thoughts. Doubt is the starting place for everyone who confronts these questions. Perhaps you will find this book worth considering if you can remain open to those possibilities. Despite appearances, there is hope for our nation and for us individually.

Cross Roads

Contents

Dedication iv

Acknowledgments v

Preface vi

Who or What Are We? 1

Mankind's Primal Wrong Turn 3

Israel and America: Twins or Cousins? 5

America's Birth Certificate 11

Factions and Ideologies That Have Undermined America 17

    Education 17

    Darwinian Evolution 23

    Marxism/Communism 25

    The Rise of Communism in America 27

    Hollywood and the Entertainment Industry 33

    The U.S. Supreme Court 47

    The "News" Media 51

    The New World Order/One World Government 53

    The End Time Rulers 59

God's Counsel for Mankind 63

    Race Relations 65

    Gender and Marriage 67

    Deceitfulness 69

    Freeloading 70

    The Value of Children; Abortion 71

    Those Who Harm Children or Cause Them to Sin or Lose Faith . 72

    Morality 73

The Invisible Battle for America 75
    Confronting the Unseen 75
    Israel's Apostasy 79
When God is Expelled, What Steps In? 81
Our Invincible Hope 87
    Winning the Battle 87
Revival or Collapse? 89
    Is Your Eternal Destiny Secure? 93
Epilogue 95
About the Author 97
Bibliography and Further Resources 98

Cross Roads

Has America made too many wrong turns to find its way home?

James Downey

Cross Roads

Who or What Are We?

Centuries of studying our world, ourselves, and the cosmos around us have produced two competing answers to the questions of God's existence and human origins. One accepts the theory known as Darwinian Evolution, which asserts that all life on earth descended from a single living cell that formed millions of years ago by the random, chance, undirected coming together of non-living chemicals.

If this theory is true, then people are no more than highly-evolved animals whose existence is merely a cosmic accident. Mankind has no purpose. We are free to run our lives and do as we please, subject only to our individual or collective whims of right or wrong and whatever means we devise to limit or control human behavior. This view allows for the incorporation of humanistic ideas and philosophical musings to make sense of the world. It also allows one to believe that physical death is no more than "lights out." Our brief existence on earth is all that we will ever experience.

The Biblical worldview holds that the heavens, the earth, and all living things on Earth were created by God and that the Bible is God's inspired word. If this worldview is true, there is reason and purpose for our existence, and an infinitely higher power to whom we are accountable, as well as standards of right or wrong defined by our Creator, not us. The God of the Bible is above human comprehension, supremely powerful, and exists eternally beyond space and time. Physical death is the doorway to an eternal destiny that will be either incredibly beautiful or unimaginably horrible. Thankfully, we can choose where we will spend eternity.

Scores of books, college courses, and internet sites thoroughly discuss and dissect the many theistic and non-theistic worldviews available for our selection. Over many years, as a trained skeptic attorney, I have weighed and compared the manifold schools of thought that seek to explain life and its meaning. Philosophy, psychology, sociology, anthropology, and the multiplicity of religions all contribute interesting ideas. Science tries to make the case that it can explain everything. But ultimately, only one hypothesis can hold all things together.

The rectitude of the Biblical worldview, the one I have settled upon, is bolstered by several external and internal factors. Some appear solid beyond serious dispute. Recent biological discoveries prove that the irreducible complexity of cellular activity and the information systems necessary to control it, such as DNA and RNA, render the theory of Darwinian Evolution a mathematical impossibility. Historical evidence, together with what my eyes, ears, and heart tell me, plus the remarkable occurrence of hundreds of precisely-described events foretold in the Bible centuries before they occurred, substantiate the validity of the Bible as God's word. And yes, irrespective of the objective evidence, faith is essential to belief, which is a choice presented to each of us. That choice will, consciously or subconsciously, inform our paths through life.

Mankind's Primal Wrong Turn

Adam and Eve, the first two people God created, lived in the Garden of Eden with trees that were *pleasing to the eye and good for food* (Genesis 2:9.) Mankind was meant to live in a close, eternal relationship with God. Among the abilities gifted to mankind was the free will to make choices, good or bad.

To establish and emphasize His authority, God gave Adam a command. Adam was forbidden to eat the fruit of one specific tree in the garden, the tree of the knowledge of good and evil. Adam was warned that if he disobeyed, he would *certainly die* (Genesis 2:17.) Eve was made aware of God's command.

Ideally, had Adam and Eve simply obeyed God, they could have set the stage for a proper relationship between God and the rest of mankind. But God's adversary, Satan (the devil,) was also present in the Garden. Appearing to Eve in the form of a serpent, Satan deceived Eve and tempted her to eat from the forbidden fruit. Eve chose to disobey God's command and ate some. She then gave the fruit to Adam, who ate as well.

God confronted Adam, Eve, and the serpent, pronouncing punishments that would burden them as well as all generations to follow. Adam and Eve's fellowship with God was broken, and they were barred from eating the fruit of the tree of life that would have enabled them to live forever (Genesis 3:22-24.) Adam's choice to disobey God introduced physical and spiritual death for all mankind.

Adam and Eve were expelled from the garden. They, and their descendants, were condemned to work the soil for their food, battling thorns, thistles, and the weary work of farming. Women would experience pain in child birth. Because of Adam's sin, every person is born afflicted with an inherent sin nature akin to a genetic defect that separates us from God and His Holiness.

The turmoil of our present condition flows from God's proclamation to the serpent: . . . *I will put enmity* (positive, active mutual hatred and ill will) *between you and the woman, and between your offspring and hers; . . .* (Genesis 3:15.) Each of us is born into this overarching conflict between good and evil, God and Satan.

Mercifully, God provided mankind the means to reconcile with Him two-thousand years ago, enabling us to overcome physical death and spend eternity in Heaven. But we must choose that path. Unless we do so, our physical demise and eternal destiny end very badly.

Israel and America: Twins or Cousins?

Israel and America are considered the only two nations founded upon a dedication to God. Israel was born four-thousand years ago when God made a series of covenant promises to a man named Abraham, who found favor with God because of his strong faith. Abraham would become the father of countless descendants, set apart from all other nations as God's chosen people. One of his descendants (Jesus) would bless the entire world.

Although Europeans from Spain and other countries began exploring America and established some settlements here before 1620, it is widely considered that America's foundation stone was laid some four hundred years ago when Pilgrims from England established the Massachusetts Colony in 1620, in their own words, . . . *for the Glory of God, and Advancement of the Christian Faith* . . . (Mayflower Compact.)

The unequivocal dedication of that colony to God, our infusion of Biblical principles into our founding and governing documents, and our reliance upon Him to sustain us for a significant part of our history created a kinship with Israel that invites comparisons.

Centuries after the birth of Abraham's first son Isaac, a famine drove the nation of Israel to migrate to Egypt. As the population of Israel increased dramatically, Egypt's leader became fearful that Israel's growing numbers posed a threat to Egypt's dominance. The Egyptians subdued and brutally enslaved Israel, keeping the nation captive for four hundred years.

The Israelis cried out to God for deliverance. God heard Israel's cries and chose a man named Moses to lead Israel out of its captivity. After visiting plagues and catastrophes upon Egypt to force its ruler to release the Israelis, in 1446 B.C., God led over one million of them to an encampment in the desert. God began handing down to Moses the laws that would govern Israel from then forward, including Israel's foundational Covenant:

> *Then Moses went up to God, and the Lord called to him from the mountain and said, "This is what you are to say to the descendants of Jacob [Abraham's grandson] and what you are to tell the people of Israel: 'You yourselves have seen what I did to Egypt, and how I carried you on eagles' wings and brought you to myself. Now if you obey me fully and keep my covenant, then out of all nations you will be my treasured possession. Although the whole earth is mine, you will be for me a kingdom of priests and a holy nation.' These are the words you are to speak to the Israelites"* (Exodus 19:3-6.)

To receive God's blessings, Israel was obligated to obey God fully and keep His covenants.

God's first laws, the "Ten Commandments," set Israel apart from the pagan nations surrounding it who worshipped multiple gods and man-made idols. The first law commanded: *you shall have no other gods before Me.* The second declared:

*You shall not make for yourself any idol or any likeness of what is in heaven above or on the earth beneath or in the water under the earth [*as an object of worship.*] You shall not worship them nor serve them;* . . . (Exodus 20:2-5, Amplified Bible.)

Over the next thousand years, Israel alternated between periods of worshipping and obeying God and keeping His covenants and times of apostasy when it turned to pagan rituals. During the times of obedience, Israel enjoyed peace, prosperity, and miraculous military victories. When Israel turned from God and began worshipping man-made idols, the multiple gods associated with them, and engaging in pagan rituals, including consorting with temple prostitutes and even child sacrifice by fire, Israel suffered crushing military defeats, the banishment of its citizens into captivity within conquering nations, destruction of Jerusalem, and dispersions of its people among surrounding nations.

God exhibited remarkable patience with Israel, giving the nation ample time to correct its ways. Before imposing each judgment, God sent a prophet through Israel [an individual ordained and chosen from among its people] to chastise the Israelis for their disobedience and to warn them that failure to repent and return to Him would bring punishment. Israel frequently ignored these warnings and even persecuted some of the prophets. The Bible identifies seventeen prophets.

Is America following Israel's pattern of apostasy, turning away from God in favor of idols* such as money, fame, power, success, material possessions, and sexual gratification, and banishing Him and His word from our schools, halls of government, and any form of public mention? Was 9-11 a warning from God of things to come if we continue down this path? Do Israel's beginnings and misguided journeys foreshadow a similar fate for America?

>*1 Corinthians 10:14, Amplified Bible: *Therefore, my beloved, run [keep far, far away] from [any sort of] idolatry [and that includes loving anything more than God, or participating in anything that leads to sin and enslaves the soul].*
>
>*Colossians 3:5, Amplified Bible: *So put to death and deprive of power the evil longings of your earthly body [with its sensual, self-centered instincts], immorality, impurity, sinful passion, evil desire, and greed, which is [a kind of] idolatry [because it replaces your devotion to God].*

America's duplication of Israel's pattern of apostasy is not the only reason to conclude that America may be experiencing similar judgment. God's hand bears upon all nations regardless of whether they acknowledge or honor Him.

>Psalm 47:8: *God reigns over the nations; God is seated on his holy throne.*
>
>Psalm 22:28: . . . *for dominion belongs to the Lord, and he rules over the nations.*
>
>Psalm 33:12-15: *Blessed is the nation whose God is the Lord, the people he chose for his inheritance. From Heaven the Lord looks down and sees all mankind;*

from his dwelling place, he watches all who live on earth—he who forms the hearts of all, who considers everything they do.

The Zondervan *NIV Study Bible's* marginal comments note: *The principle described here is true for individuals, families, communities and even entire nations: those who serve God will benefit from their close relationship with him. This specific promise in its context, however, applied to Israel—the nation chosen as God's inheritance.*

Psalm 110:6: *He will judge the nations, heaping up the dead and crushing the rulers of the whole earth.*

Psalm 66:7: *He rules forever by his power, his eyes watch the nations—let not the rebellious rise up against him.*

Proverbs 11:14: :*For lack of guidance, a nation falls.*

Proverbs 14:34: *Righteousness exalts a nation, but sin condemns any people.*

Jeremiah 46:28 (God announcing Babylon's coming conquest of Egypt to His prophet Jeremiah): *"Do not be afraid Jacob [Israel] my servant, for I am with you," declares the Lord. "Though I completely destroy all the nations among which I scatter you, I will not completely destroy you. I will discipline you but only in due measure; I will not let you go entirely unpunished."*

God applies the same measures to individuals as well as to nations. Faith and obedience bring blessings, while sin brings consequences and judgment.

To appreciate how far our country has fallen, we need only compare its present social norms with those prevailing at the time of its founding and during its earlier years.

America's Birth Certificate

England's colonization of America was preceded by explorations and the establishment of a few settlements by other nations, including Spain. Over time, England became the dominant colonial power until America's Declaration of Independence.

England's first colony in America was founded in Jamestown, Virginia, in 1607. In 1620, the *Mayflower* sailed from England carrying some one hundred Separatists from the Church of England, known as Pilgrims, seeking freedom to worship unshackled from the requirements of that church. Although the Pilgrims were not the first colonists to arrive, they are largely credited with establishing America's Biblical foundation.

England's King Henry VIII seized control of the English church in 1534, sparking decades of deadly conflict between Roman Catholics and Protestants. A succession of Kings and Queens sided back and forth with one faction or the other until Queen Elizabeth I gained the throne and redesigned the church, attempting to blend Catholic and Protestant doctrines and practices as a compromise. This satisfied some, yet the Separatists maintained that the blended governance and liturgy strayed far from the Bible. English law prohibited them from practicing their faith outside of the Church of England. One congregation fled to Holland to escape persecution, but this proved to be unsatisfactory for several reasons, prompting them to purchase passage to North America on the *Mayflower*.

The *Mayflower* held a Patent from England authorizing its colonists to settle in one specific location: Virginia. Wind and sea conditions and navigation issues prevented them from reaching Virginia, forcing them to drop anchor and come ashore in Provincetown near Cape Cod, Massachusetts.

Faced with the dilemma of having no official permission to colonize where they landed, they crafted an agreement known as the "Mayflower Compact," establishing themselves as a self-governing entity. Its preamble reads:

> *IN THE NAME OF GOD, AMEN. We, whose names are underwritten, the Loyal Subjects of our dread Sovereign Lord King James, by the Grace of God, of Great Britain, France and Ireland, King, Defender of the Faith &c. Having undertaken for the Glory of God, and Advancement of the Christian Faith, and the Honour (sic) of our King and Country, a Voyage to plant the first Colony in the northern Parts of Virginia; do by these Presents, solemnly and mutually, in the presence of God and one another, covenant and combine ourselves into a civil Body Politick (sic) . . .*

America grew and expanded into its original thirteen colonies. The documents establishing and governing our colonies, our Declaration of Independence, and our Constitution and Bill of Rights, are infused with Biblical principles and acknowledgment of God as the bedrock of our nation. Throughout our early history and the Civil War era, America's leaders continued to acknowledge our reliance upon God and his provenance to sustain our nation. They warned us that, should America stray from its faith and founding Biblical principles, our country would likely disintegrate.

Emma Hart Willard (1787—1870), the author of numerous books and textbooks, a pioneer in education for women, and the founder and curator of the Troy Female Seminary in 1821, whose writings were . . . *well received by such readers as Thomas Jefferson and John Adams,* affirmed these principles in 1843:

> *The government of the United States is acknowledged by the wise and good of other nations, to be the most free, impartial and righteous government in the world; but all agree, that for such a government to be sustained for many years, the principles of truth and righteousness taught in the Holy Scriptures, must be practised (sic). The rulers must govern in the fear of God, and the people obey the laws* (from *Teaching and Learning America's Christian History.*)

Our Declaration of Independence acknowledges God as the author and sustainer of our freedom:

> 1. Natural law is the only proper basis for a sound government, that being, . . . *the separate and equal station to which the Laws of Nature and Nature's God entitle [*people to govern themselves by*]*
>
> 2. *We [*the authors of the Declaration*] hold these truths to be self-evident, that all men are created equal, that they are endowed by their Creator with certain unalienable Rights . . .*

> 3. *We, therefore, the representatives of the United States of America, in general Congress assembled, appealing to the Supreme Judge of the world for rectitude of our intentions, do . . . solemnly publish and declare that these united colonies are . . . free and independent states; . . . [dissolving] . . . all political connection between them and the State of Great Britain . . . And for the support of this declaration, with a firm reliance on the protection of Divine Providence, we mutually pledge to each other our lives, our fortunes, and our sacred honor.*

As recently as 1954, during our "Cold War" with the Soviet Union, the words "under God" were added to America's Pledge of Allegiance. We declared we were "one nation under God," in rebuttal to that Communist nation's open embrace of atheism. Our coinage continues to bear the words, "In God We Trust."

Within recent years, a very high-level public official disingenuously quipped that America is not a Christian nation. Had he been truthful, he would have said that we are "no longer" a Christian nation since many have worked long and hard to erase our foundation and any public acknowledgment of it. In later sections, excerpts are included from an extensive two-volume collection of our historic governing documents and quotes from our early founders confirming America's bedrock of Biblical principles. Written in the 1960s, *The Christian History of the Constitution of the United States of*

America and *Teaching and Learning America's Christian History,* produced by The Foundation for American Christian Education, are essential components to any effort to accurately teach or learn American history.

How did a country created upon such a firm foundation deteriorate into what we see today?

Cross Roads

Factions and Ideologies That Have Undermined America

Education

Today's education of children differs significantly from our colonial period and earlier days as a nation. In the 17th and 18th centuries, children were not generally required to attend school, nor were communities required to provide schools for them. At that time, children were typically taught by their parents or tutors. Some entered trade apprenticeships, receiving on-the-job training.

The Puritans of Massachusetts originated the purposeful schooling of children. As the population of non-Puritans increased in the Massachusetts Colony, the Puritans remained influenced by their memories of the religious persecution they fled England to escape, the need to maintain a solid Biblical foundation to sustain the growing colonies and their deep belief in the value of literacy.

In 1642, they passed our first law requiring parents to educate their children. This was followed in 1647 by "The Old Deluder Satan Act," mandating some towns to build schools. It aimed to counter its namesake's tactic of keeping people ignorant of the Scriptures.

Before publishing facilities were established, the Geneva Bible was used by the colonists to teach reading. Children were taught literacy and Biblical knowledge together until the 1690s when the first published reading textbook appeared.

Continuing our practice of teaching Biblical principles, *The New England Primer* was filled with Bible passages. Our founding fathers from New England and beyond, including Samuel Adams, Benjamin Franklin, John Adams, John Hancock, and Paul Revere, were weaned on the principles provided in some measure by this book.

Colonial colleges were primarily focused on training men as ministers before 1800. Several of today's colleges and universities were established as religious institutions, a fact many find ironic considering what is being taught to today's college students.

Harvard was founded by the colonial legislature in 1636, initially training ministers. The College of William and Mary was established by Virginia's government in 1693, closely affiliated with the Anglican Church. Yale was started by the Puritans in 1701, based upon some dissatisfaction with Harvard's more liberal theology. In 1747, New Side Presbyterians established the College of New Jersey in Princeton, now known as Princeton University. The Anglicans developed Kings College in New York City in 1746, which later became Columbia University.

Massachusetts resident Horace Mann had a significant influence on public education that persists today. After the American Revolution, Thomas Jefferson argued in favor of a tax-supported education system, but the idea did not gain much traction until Horace Mann appeared on the scene. Mann, born in 1796, did not enjoy an affluent life. Early teachers provided minimal education. He was largely self-educated, studying books available in the Franklin,

Massachusetts town library and receiving Latin and Greek tutoring from Samuel Barrett, who later became a leading Unitarian Minister.

Admitted to Brown University in 1816, Mann exhibited an interest in politics, education, and social reform. After attending law school, he served in the Massachusetts House of Representatives, the state's Senate, and later in the U.S. House of Representatives. While in the Massachusetts legislature, he strongly advocated for state control of education, which he felt had deteriorated under economy-driven local school districts. His efforts, together with those of like-minded reformers, resulted in the establishment of a State Board of Education in 1837. He accepted the first secretaryship of the Board. Mann crafted and advocated six principles he claimed were essential for public education:

1. Universal public education is necessary because a republic cannot long remain ignorant and free.

2. Such education must be paid for, controlled, and sustained by an interested public.

3. Education should be *profoundly moral in character* but free of sectarian religious influence.

4. Education must be permeated throughout by the spirit, methods, and discipline of a free society, which precludes harsh pedagogy in the classroom.

5. Education can only be provided by well-trained, professional teachers.

6. Schools should embrace children of all religious, social, and ethnic backgrounds.

Some of Mann's ideas were opposed by clergymen who thought Biblical principles were essential to sound curricula, by educators who felt his pedagogy subverted classroom authority, and by those who opposed the state usurping local educational authority. It is unclear where Mann expected any "profound moral character" in public education to come from, given his exclusion of sectarian religious content. Mann's ideas seem to have prevailed over his critics.

Mann has been christened by some as "The Father of American Education." His ideal public-education policy of excluding sectarian instruction foreshadowed the U.S. Supreme Court decisions in 1962 and 1963 prohibiting prayer and Bible reading in public schools.

The shift of our public-school curricula from teaching core academic subjects such as math, reading, science, history, and civics, to implementing political and social indoctrination and revisionist distortions of history did not occur by happenstance. A group of influential Americans met in New York City in 1905 for the express purpose of replacing the country's prevailing Christian world view with Marxism (Communism.)

Part of their strategy was to populate the education system with those sympathetic to and willing to actively promote that agenda. The organizations they founded to accomplish this have now permeated most spheres of influence in America (see the section entitled "The Rise of Communism in America.") Their efforts were boosted by the above-referenced Supreme Court rulings, launching a series of decisions by that Court which succeeded in eliminating any vestiges of our Christian founding and Biblical content from public schools (see the section entitled "The U.S. Supreme Court.")

Sadly, according to author Verna M. Hall, our Biblical foundations have not been taught in Christian schools for some time:

> *. . . America's Christian history has not been taught in Christian schools and colleges for over one hundred years. This fact has contributed to the rise of secularism—the "irreligious" spirit—more than any other single educational factor. . . . As Americans and as Christians have moved away from the teaching of history from its original sources they have accepted the interpretations of those who deal with history "seeing only secondary causes and human agencies."* [Quoting Rev. A.W. Foljambe, January 5, 1876]. *The result has been our separation of history from God as the Author of History* (from *Teaching and Learning America's History*.)

School shootings in the U.S. have been cited as evidence of what happens when God is eliminated from our schools.

Statistically, this is likely accurate, although U.S. school shootings are not a new phenomenon. *Wikipedia* has chronicled them since 1840 (including accidental shootings.) From 1840 through 1899, a total of 33 occurred. 1900 through 1949 saw a total of 55. By decade thereafter: 1950s: 19; 1960s: 20; 1970s: 42; 1980s: 62; 1990s: 99. However, the nature of more recent shootings, such as the Columbine incident in Colorado, signal a severe moral decline in our culture. When human life is deemed to have no purpose or value, what else can be expected?

More telling is the last few years. For the sake of propriety, the activities and doctrines being forced upon our children in many public schools will not be described. They promote division, discord, and sexual agendas vehemently opposed by the overwhelming majority. They have no place in our schools yet have found their way into the void left by our expulsion of God from our schools and the public sphere. Citizens in several locales have recalled their school boards in response to these trends. Is any more needed to awaken us?

Darwinian Evolution

Charles Darwin, 1809—1882, of the United Kingdom, pioneered the theory of evolution, offering his explanation of how today's biological species came about. Darwin's ideas have led to the substitution of the altar of science for the Biblical account of creation once prevalent in America.

Wikipedia publishes the following blurb purporting to tell people who Darwin was and what he is noted for: Charles Darwin was *an English naturalist, geologist, and biologist widely known for contributing to evolutionary biology. His proposition that all species of life have descended from a common ancestor **is now generally accepted and considered a fundamental concept in science*** (emphasis supplied.)

Two books written by Darwin describe his thinking. *Voyage of the Beagle,* 1839, chronicles his shipboard journeys during which he collected biological specimens. *On the Origin of Species,* 1859, expands upon what he found on those journeys to propose a relatively novel (at that time) theory of the evolution of species.

The present iteration of this theory claims that millions of years ago, non-living chemicals randomly came together by pure chance, undirected by any outside agency, to form a single living cell that evolved to produce the multiple thousands of plant and animal species present today.

Darwin's theory is still being taught as fact in many schools, despite the significant body of evidence in biology and other sciences that refute it, as well as the substantial number of scientists who reject it. *Wikipedia's* blurb claiming Darwin's theory is a "fundamental concept in science" is grossly misleading.

Some in America put up a fight. In 1925, the State of Tennessee filed charges against high-school teacher John Scopes for violating a state law prohibiting the teaching of evolution. Dubbed "The Scopes Monkey Trial" by someone in the media, the dispute was engineered by the American Civil Liberties Union (ACLU) to test the law's constitutionality. Criminal Defense Attorney Clarence Darrow represented Scopes (see the upcoming section "The Rise of Communism in America" for more about Darrow.) Disappointingly to the defendants, the law was ultimately upheld by the Tennessee Supreme Court.

The issue spawned a series of legal actions that culminated in 1987 with a U.S. Supreme Court decision crowning evolution the winner, extinguishing any public-school teaching of intelligent design or creation, even as competing theories (see the section entitled "The U.S. Supreme Court.")

Marxism/Communism

Karl Marx (1818-1883) is known as the father of Communism (a/k/a Marxism, Liberalism, or Progressivism.) Dictionary definitions of "Communism" range from the idyllic: a system in which goods are owned in common and are available to all as needed, to the far more accurate: a totalitarian system of government in which a single authoritarian party controls state-owned means of production.

The global spread of Communism has fostered untold human misery and millions of deaths caused by the regimes that have adopted and enslaved their citizens under that form of government. Common to both Darwinism and Marxism is a rejection of what the Bible teaches, as well as disparagement and persecution of those who adhere to Biblical beliefs.

Marx co-authored the *Communist Manifesto* with Friedrich Engels in 1848, followed by *Das Kapital* in 1867. One of Marx's better-known platitudes is, "religion is the opiate of the masses," simply one more tool to oppress workers and make them feel better in their oppression.

Communist regimes promise a "workers' paradise" for "the people" but inevitably produce suffering, oppression, and death. There is no country where Communism has produced anything positive for "the people," the masses whom it purportedly champions.

While immigrants swarm across our borders by the thousands, we have yet to witness multitudes crashing the borders of the likes of Communist China, North Korea, Russia, Cuba, or Venezuela. Since Russia's Communist revolution in 1917, it is estimated that its various leaders are responsible for eighty-five million deaths through genocide, murder, starvation, and famines produced by their hopelessly-flawed attempts to bring everything, including food production, under government control. In contrast, the total number of worldwide deaths attributed to WWII is sixty million. Communist regimes suppress and persecute Christians, who are seen as a threat to their totalitarian rule, as well as everyone who stands for the truth or dares to challenge their abuses of power. Anyone who thinks this could never happen in America needs to awaken to the repression already occurring here.

The Rise of Communism in America

The depths and early inception of the concerted effort to convert America to a Communist regime are startling. In 1905, a faction of influential Americans enamored with Marx and his writings met for this specific purpose. The names and stations in business, education, and government of those who founded and those who later joined the organizations promoting this effort are breathtaking and disheartening. The list includes at least one Supreme Court justice. We are witnessing today the fruits of this century-plus effort to destroy the country our founders created.

A CASE STUDY IN CHANGING A NATION'S CULTURE

Its membership was relatively small, but its influence continues today.

On September 12, 1905, approximately one hundred people met in a loft over Peck's Restaurant at 140 Fulton Street in lower Manhattan. The purpose of the meeting was to strategize the overthrow of the Christian worldview that still pervaded much of American culture and to replace it with the ideas of a then rather unknown writer by the name of Karl Marx. They called the organization they formed that day the Intercollegiate Socialist Society.

The godfather of the organization was a twenty-seven-year-old author named Upton. Sinclair. The first president chosen was the author Jack London. Also present was Clarence Darrow, the attorney.

The strategy of the organization was to infiltrate their ideas into academia by organizing chapters in as many colleges and universities as possible. And organize they did. Walter Lippman, later author and director of the Council of Foreign Relations, was the president of the Harvard chapter. Walter Reuther, the future president of the United Auto Workers, headed the Wayne State chapter; and Eugene Debs, who went on to become the five-time Socialist candidate for president, was a leader at Columbia.

The society grew. The first annual convention was held in 1910, and by 1917 they were active on sixty-one campuses and a dozen graduate schools. Other early activists included W.E.B. DuBois, who would become an official of the NAACP and later a Communist Party member, and Victor L. Berger of Wisconsin, who became the first Socialist elected to Congress.

In 1921 the Intercollegiate Socialists Society took its next organizational step, changing its name to the League for Industrial Democracy. Its purpose was "education for a new social order based on production for use and not for profit." Norman Thomas, another perennial Socialist candidate for president, was the leader behind the scenes. The renamed organization's first president was Robert Lovett, editor of the New Republic, *and the field secretary was Paul Blanshard, who later became an author.*

The college chapters of the Intercollegiate Socialist Society now became the Student League for Industrial Democracy. As members graduated from college, some entered the pulpit, others the classroom; some wrote textbooks while others entered the labor movement and both political parties. When the New Deal began in 1933, they were prepared. At the time the league had only 5,652 members, but they were in positions of leadership everywhere.

By 1941 John Dewey, the founder of progressive education and the league vice president in the 1930s, was its honorary president, and Reinhold Niebuhr, the theologian, its treasurer. Dewey had already organized the Progressive Education Association and the American Association of University Professors.

The League for Industrial Democracy was so successful that those who held membership in its movement or were cooperating with it could have been a list for Who's Who in America: *Robert N. Baldwin, founder of the American Civil Liberties Union; Charles Beard, the historian; Carroll Binder, editor of the* Minneapolis Tribune; *Helen Gahagan Douglas, the congresswoman who was defeated by Richard Nixon for the U.S. Senate; Felix Frankfurter, Supreme Court Justice; Sidney Hook, the educational philosopher; Edna St. Vincent Millay, the poet; Henry Morgenthau Jr., one of Franklin Delano Roosevelt's most trusted economic advisers; Walter and Victor Reuther, United Auto Workers; Will Rogers Jr., humorist; Franklin*

Roosevelt Jr., the president's son; and Arthur Schlesinger, the historian.

The obscure loft in Manhattan where they organized has long been forgotten, but what they began there that night permeates America's institutions and culture, having replaced the Bible-based values of the nineteenth century with a liberalism based on Marxism (from *The One Year Christian History.*)

Vera M. Hall, the compiler of *The Christian History of the Constitution of the United States of America* (cited above), was motivated by her observations in college and while working in government that America was headed towards inherently-atheistic socialism. In response, she . . . *left government service and began a Constitutional study group . . . in 1947.* Ms. Hall continues, *For about twenty years [I] searched for the fundamental reasons why America embarked upon a path of socialism, and why Americans continue to travel this ever-increasing and widening road.* (Her finished works were published in the 1960s).

Hall concluded that our misdirection was primarily caused by our failure to teach each generation about our founders' intentional incorporation of Biblical principles and acknowledgment of God into the documents that created our nation and form of government. This led to our replacement of God's sovereignty with that of the State, as our founding faith and knowledge of it have slowly eroded. The failure to teach these principles has not been solely from neglect. A conscious effort to prevent their teaching has played a major role.

Ms. Hall notes the warning we were given 2,000 years ago in Colossians 2:8, Amplified Bible:

> *See to it that no one takes you captive through philosophy and empty deception [pseudo-intellectual babble], according to the tradition [and musings] of mere men, following the elementary principles of this world, rather than following [the truth—the teachings of] Christ.*

For those unfamiliar with Communism and its corrosive results, a study of an honest recitation of its motives, means, objectives, and the countries it has devastated is essential. If we cannot understand the direction in which our country is headed, America will join the list of nations that Communism has ruined.

Cross Roads

Hollywood and the Entertainment Industry

The captivating story of Hollywood's founder, Hobart Johnstone ("HJ") Whitley (1847-1931), exemplifies one major wrong turn when America decided it could simultaneously maintain its Biblical principles while racing after its endless opportunities for wealth and success, the "shiny objects" produced by fascinating new technologies, and enjoying the pleasures of loosening social and moral restraints. One could scarcely find a more poignant lesson in how well-intentioned, morally grounded people can be enticed to participate in and promote something their instincts warn them will likely cause a wide-spread corruption of prevailing values.

I was introduced to HJ by a book entitled *The Father of Hollywood,* written by his great-granddaughter, Gaelyn Whitley Keith. HJ was almost single-handedly responsible for the birth of Hollywood, CA, as a city and its development as the entertainment capital of the world.

After the death of his first wife, HJ's second wife, Gigi, maintained an extensive journal chronicling their life together, from the time of their marriage in 1886 through and somewhat beyond the year HJ passed away, 1931.

HJ and Gigi came from cultured, accomplished, and prosperous families. They shared a firm knowledge of God as well as an adherence to the refined culture and social norms of their time, although Gigi was supportive of the emerging women's rights movement that brought about the 19th Amendment to the U.S. Constitution granting women the right to vote.

Visionary entrepreneur HJ acquired skills, knowledge, and abilities through formal education as well as self-directed studies. He also possessed an innate charm enabling him to connect with and influence most everyone he met.

In 1865, within weeks of each other, two tragic events marred HJ's life. First, his parents were killed when the horse-drawn buggy they were driving was struck by a train. Shortly thereafter came the assassination of President Abraham Lincoln. Later in his life, HJ's first wife and child were killed in a house fire started by a candle that ignited a window curtain. These events seem to have had a lasting effect on his ongoing years that fueled his drive to pursue serial business ventures and success.

Bolstered by his degree from Toronto (Canada) Business College, HJ entered the business world and enjoyed early success. In search of broader horizons, he moved to Chicago, where he increased his finances by opening a grocery and dry goods mercantile business. His desire for adventure and even greater opportunities led him to embrace America's booming "Go West Young Man" frenzy.

The railroads' massive push into America's new Western frontiers, combined with his increasing wealth and self-education in civil engineering, enabled him to acquire properties and develop towns along the Rock Island Railroad's westward expansion through the Dakotas, Nebraska, Iowa, Kansas, Oklahoma, Colorado, and Texas. Between 1870 and 1890, HJ established over one hundred towns, including Wichita and Emporia in Kansas, Stillwater and Norman in

Oklahoma, and Humboldt in Iowa. His business acquisitions and endeavors expanded into banking, land development, and mortgage companies. By any measure, HJ became an extremely wealthy man.

A chance meeting on a train in 1885 brought then-38-year-old HJ and then 18-year-old Gigi, who was traveling with her uncle as her escort, together. After an ensuing courtship, HJ and Gigi were married in 1886. Their honeymoon took them to Los Angeles, described in Gigi's journal as it had appeared to her in 1885 on the trip with her uncle, thusly: . . . *inhabited by fewer than sixty thousand people. Not much more than the remains of an adobe Spanish settlement . . . The roads were primitive. I found riding in the [*horse-drawn*] carriage difficult because of all the dust the horses stirred up in the rainless weather on those bumpy trails.*

While in LA, the couple became acquainted with General Harrison Gray Otis, a Civil War veteran and co-founder of *The Los Angeles Times* newspaper. Otis was familiar with HJ's development work and sought to persuade HJ to join him in developing Southern California's seemingly endless open spaces. Otis invited the couple to look around the area. HJ and Gigi rented horses, packed a lunch, and proceeded to explore. They traveled North for a time, spellbound by the natural beauty around them.

Drawn by the panoramic views promised at the top of a mountain, the couple began the trek towards its summit. HJ stopped to make sketches in his notebook to better recall later his thoughts towards the development potential for a town. He and Gigi spied a Chinese man driving a rickety one-horse wagon loaded with wood *pell-mell down the narrow road.* The man stopped by them. When HJ asked the man what he was doing, he replied that he was gathering wood from trees that he said had *fallen down,* exclaiming, *Pick up wood. All time hauly wood.* According to the book, this is where and how HJ decided upon the name for the new town he intended to develop . . . *among these beautiful hills. Hollywood.*

General Otis tried to persuade HJ to remain in California, but HJ had ongoing business elsewhere that he needed to return to. Before leaving, HJ secured his future right to purchase 500 acres for his new town, Hollywood.

HJ and Gigi traveled to the Dakotas, where HJ had established a home while participating in local ventures. In 1889, the Oklahoma Territory was opened for settlement and land acquisition. HJ and Gigi relocated there while HJ acquired and developed several land holdings in which he built brick and stone banks and other buildings, which were usually the first buildings made of that material in the towns. After declining the offered governorship of Oklahoma, he accepted the nomination as president of the Chamber of Commerce of its first capital, Guthrie. He also traveled to Washington, DC, to help establish laws governing the Oklahoma Territory.

Fulfilling their dream to settle permanently in California, HJ and Gigi purchased a stately three-story home in Los Angeles in 1894. Perhaps as a harbinger, the first showing of a motion picture took place that year in New York.

HJ encountered some unfortunate delays and obstacles in closing his option to purchase the land for his residential development. In the interim, he opened a jewelry store in Los Angeles that rivaled the finest in New York City and enjoyed immediate success. He and Gigi traveled to Europe regularly to purchase gems and other items for their store. In 1899, HJ finally closed his purchase of the optioned residential land, reduced by circumstances to 480 acres, composed of a single hill located North of Hollywood Boulevard overlooking present-day Hollywood.

From the time of his arrival, he began encouraging people to use the name "Hollywood" for his new town. His 480-acre residential subdivision, Whitley Heights, was comparable to today's Beverly Hills. It became the first situs of stately homes that housed Hollywood's rising movie stars, including Charlie Chaplin, Rudolph Valentino, and W.C. Fields. (In 1948, Whitley Heights was cut in two by the construction of the Hollywood Freeway, n/k/a locally as "the 101." The westerly portion of the subdivision was placed on the National Register of Historic Places in 1982 after years of efforts to preserve it from commercial development and demolition of its historic homes to make way for new construction).

During HJ's earlier years in Hollywood, its infrastructure was in dire need of improvement. HJ initiated plans to locate and construct a high school, provide public transit, and repair, upgrade, and expand the road system. One of his new roads, aptly named "Sunset Boulevard," provided a westerly route to the beach. Many of the country's new inventions, such as electric lights, telephones, urban electric cars, and the automobile, were welcomed. Hollywood's climate and scenic open spaces provided ample opportunities for filming the newly-created form of entertainment known as moving pictures, particularly the popular "Westerns."

In addition to progress, the turn of the new century also witnessed tragedy with the assassination of U.S. President McKinley in 1901. This propelled HJ's good friend Teddy Roosevelt into the presidency.

HJ opened his self-designed Hollywood Hotel in 1902, an enormous and grand resort located at the corner of Hollywood Boulevard and Highland Avenue that became a center for *civic and social life* as well as *the home of many of the stars over the years.* The hotel was expanded by additions in later years. Its ceilings were adorned with golden stars bearing the names of famous movie celebrities. (The building stood until it was scheduled to be torn down in 1956. The pending loss of the historic ceiling stars prompted the creation of the Hollywood sidewalk known as the "Walk of Stars" that still exists, recreating many of the ceiling stars).

As his development activities continued, HJ and others organized the Bank of Hollywood that same year. Ten thousand trees and shrubs were planted by HJ to beautify the city. When it was finally incorporated in 1903, an ordinance was passed to control the herding of livestock through its streets. Saloons and *kindred evils* were unknown to Hollywood at the time, as HJ had implemented deed of trust restrictions disallowing such businesses. In 1904 Hollywood voters banned liquor from the city except as sold for medicinal purposes.

HJ, Gigi, and the early residents of Hollywood sought to maintain a moral fabric and high standards for the town. But the winds of change were highlighted by HJ's children. When their son Ross was sixteen, he was caught in his room with some friends who were smoking. Their daughter Grace discovered boys and started her teen rebellion. *Grace's skirts gradually rose scandalously to her ankles . . . but the final outrage for HJ was when he shamelessly saw her kissing in public.*

Hollywood High School was built in 1910. It opened *just as the formerly quiet village of Hollywood was being overrun by movie producers.* Was this the turning point for Hollywood's peaceful, small-town demeanor, or were the seeds sown in earlier years? Perhaps an omen for coming changes to America, in October of that year, two brothers, John J. and James B. McNamara, militant unionists, set off a dynamite bomb by the side of the *Los Angeles Times* building, killing twenty-one people. Famed attorney Clarence Darrow was hired by the union to defend them. According to one article, Darrow came to realize they were guilty and plea-bargained them to prison terms, avoiding the death penalty. Between 1907 and 1911, America sustained the longest period of terrorism in its history, with over 200 bombings taking place (from *Deadly Times.*)

Gigi wrote that the 1910 Christmas celebration perhaps marked the end to the tranquil times Hollywood enjoyed in its earliest years. *As I look towards the New Year, I realized that there were many challenges facing us, which, once accomplished and finalized, would change the face of Hollywood forever.*

The flood of movie producers into Hollywood followed HJ's fifteen-year multi-million-dollar effort to develop and beautify the town. In 1911, David and William Horsley and Al Christie produced Hollywood's first movie. HJ met David by chance on the street one day and helped David locate an address he was having trouble finding. A conversation ensued, and when HJ found that David was seeking to make a movie, HJ *immediately realized* the potential for Hollywood to take the fledgling movie industry to the next levels and beyond. HJ offered his home to film some of the scenes and provided support to David in other respects. David's studio achieved success, and soon other studios were drawn to Hollywood. Gigi noted that Hollywood audiences were *mesmerized* by the motion picture revolution. This hypnotic effect of visual media has since grown to discomforting levels.

To satisfy the public's growing fascination, some 20,000 movie theatres soon blossomed across the country. By the 1920s, millions of Americans were avid, regular theatre-goers, and Hollywood had established itself as the motion picture capital. From 1910 to 1920, Hollywood grew from a small enclave of 5,000 people to a city of 35,000.

The rapid growth of movie studios generated unanticipated social concerns. HJ and Gigi endeavored to maintain the moral and peaceful character of Hollywood. The influx of young, beautiful girls looking for stardom led to the establishment of The Studio Club, a low-cost housing and meal-providing facility, to provide a safer place for these necessities rather than leaving the girls wandering about to search for them. Over the years, its residents included ZaSu Pitts, Myrna Loy, Dorothy Malone, and Marilyn Monroe.

Business and store owners expressed alarm that the cinema invasion would corrupt their town. Gigi reports that *Many store owners along the busy boulevards put up signs in the window saying, "No dogs or actors allowed."*

Even the ever-optimistic HJ realized a problem was developing by 1921, with hordes descending on the town seeking fame and fortune. Five additional automobile agencies had opened. HJ convinced the Chamber of Commerce to publish a warning to the newcomers to beware of trying to break into the movies, as so very few succeed. More specifically, as to the chances for success, the warning noted that *Out of 100,000 persons who started at the bottom, only five reached the top.* The Central Casting Company was created to prevent the newcomers' exploitation and to provide a place for registration of the many hopefuls flocking to town seeking work as extras. Studios could obtain extras from the company at no cost to the struggling newcomers.

Gigi provided a hauntingly prescient description of the power of moving pictures to influence the mind. Describing D.W. Griffith's *Orphans of the Storm*, she wrote: *. . . spirited camera work, exaggerated emotion, and unrelenting editing, he commanded how I should feel and refused to let me judge history for myself.*

Although HJ and Gigi were among the wealthiest and most influential and successful couples in Hollywood, members of the upper elite of its society, Gigi succumbed to the hypnotic allure that movie stars enjoyed and projected. They seemingly towered above the rest of society, including the rich and famous, untouchable.

> *I became fascinated with the film stars. . . . I would see glamorous Hollywood stars at premiers, the best parties, restaurants and charity functions. At times, they seemed mysterious and inaccessible. I realized that many of the stories I had heard about them were invented by the studios as publicity. Yet, the images they painted became true in my mind. The thought of being a vamp was almost inconceivable to me, yet enticing. It was wrong, against my principles. Why was I so spellbound by them? After all, I was a good Christian woman. . . . Lowered necklines became popular. Hemlines inched up. . . . We all wanted to be like the actresses. . . . It was the decade that began Hollywood's transformation, which ultimately resulted in changing the world.*

On the other hand, HJ was not so enamored with all the glitter.

> *He . . . tolerated the stars' sometimes-seedy promotions . . . [because of] the phenomenal growth it brought to Hollywood. At times, he would ponder what effect this would have on future generations. I [Gigi] said it was only harmless fun. Movie stars' standards were not likely to influence the world. Christian standards were too engrained in the United States.*

It would be fitting to end the Whitley story here, letting the reader absorb the irony of their hopeful rationalizations that Hollywood culture could not and would not displace and eventually help to extinguish America's Christian heritage, given our present movie (and TV) offerings and the persistent cult status of entertainment stars. But a few more reflections are in order.

Amidst discussions between HJ and other local business magnates in a local smoking lounge one Saturday evening in February 1912 concerning,

> *. . . the astronomical figures of upcoming business. Heated discussions of the movie industry ensued. The next morning at church, many old-time members complained to HJ about the evils of the movie industry. One crotchety old man said, "I feel movie-going is a ploy used by the devil. Alcohol may be the worst, but movies are right up there with it. Immodesty has spread shamelessly, and they even attack the church and its ministers. What is the world coming to?"*

HJ replied, *If cinema art wants to continue drawing the public to the movies, they will soon realize that people have high ideals. The public will eventually demand higher morals and greater truth in story lines.* How has HJ's hopeful confidence in America's ability to maintain its moral standards in the face of the unrelenting flood of movie and TV titillations turned out?

Hollywood residents were not alone in these concerns. Gigi noted, *In 1911, Pennsylvania became the first state to pass a film censorship law. Most people agreed that not all movies were suitable for all audiences.*

Fearful of federal censorship developing and losing revenue, film producers adopted an industry code. The industry has since made various half-hearted attempts at self-regulation for age-appropriate content. However, the movies (and TV shows) offered for public consumption in recent years highlight the industry's success in gradually decimating social morals. Content formerly considered reprehensible is now promoted as commonplace and acceptable.

The Hollywood story showcases the power of video media, which has evolved beyond motion pictures to include TV, video/computer games, internet offerings, managed "news" broadcasts, and virtual reality to draw and even entrap people into a misleading fantasy world that caters to their baser desires. The lessons seem clear.

1. HJ's drive for his own and Hollywood's success, Hollywood's natural attractions of climate and scenic backdrops for filming, and HJ's seizing upon and promoting the financial potential of Hollywood as the center of the movie industry combined to make that happen.

2. The movie industry began an unanticipated conscious effort to erase the moral limits of society. Why it did so is open to further inquiry.

3. Movies and the behavioral excesses of the movie stars had, and still maintain, a near-hypnotic effect on America. Gigi noted, *Photoplay, the first true movie fan magazine, had debuted in 1911 and gave*

rise to the idea of a celebrity fan culture. . . . Photoplay was an escape outlet, giving many people a chance to spend a few minutes away from the everyday realities of life.

The Bible is replete with warnings against worshipping "idols." Is it not telling that we think nothing of casually using that word to describe the media and sports celebrities we fawn over and that one of our most popular TV shows is "American Idol?"

4. The lure of enormous profits overrode obvious signs that movies would challenge and erode prevailing moral limits. It was only the fear of government regulation that drove producers to rein in their rush to demolish moral boundaries. It simply slowed their efforts to a more gradual pace.

5. The assumptions that America's prevailing Biblical morals would withstand the movies' lurid content proved sadly mistaken.

Cross Roads

The U.S. Supreme Court

In bygone years, when civics and government were taught somewhat accurately in our public schools, my generation was presented with an idealistic picture of how the various branches of government functioned. The three federal branches—executive, legislative, and judicial—were designed to hold each other accountable through "checks and balances" that would prevent one branch from overstepping its limits. Our founders strived to make it impossible for our federal government to devolve into a monarchy or dictatorship. States (i.e., the people) were supposedly granted a fair measure of freedom to regulate their affairs. When I attended law school, constitutional law was taught with a blind eye to the reality of how partisan politics corrupt the decisions of the U.S. Supreme Court.

A series of decisions that began in 1962 launched America's government-sanctioned public rejection of its Biblical roots.

> *Engle v. Vitale,* 370 U.S. 421 (1962) held that school-sponsored prayer in public schools violates the establishment clause of the First Amendment. Justice Stewart, dissenting, correctly pointed out the error of the majority's reasoning. The Establishment Clause was only meant to prohibit the establishment of a state-sponsored church, such as the Church of England (whose repressions the Pilgrim settlers had fled England to escape.) *Engle* opened the door for courts to impose further restrictions upon anything Biblical being said, done, or displayed on government-affiliated premises.

Abington School District v. Schemp, 374 U.S. 203 (1963) invalidated the reading of Bible verses and recitation of the Lord's Prayer in public schools.

The Scopes Monkey Trial in 1925 was simply the opening salvo in a continuing legal war over the teaching of evolution in public schools. In *Epperson v. Arkansas* (referenced above), 393 U.S. 97 (1968), the Court struck down an Arkansas law that criminalized the teaching of evolution in public schools, citing *Abington* as a controlling authority. In response, some states enacted laws requiring the balanced teaching of evolution and creation science. The statutes requiring balanced treatment were eventually struck down in *McClean v. Arkansas,* U.S. D.Ct. E.D. Ark., 1981, and later by the U.S. Supreme Court in *Edwards v. Aguillard,* 482 U.S. 578 (1987), crowning evolution the victor in the war over what public schools can teach regarding the origins of life.

The year I graduated from law school, 1973, witnessed one of the most politically-motivated and legally-bankrupt opinions in that court's history, *Roe v. Wade*, 410 U.S. 113, which somehow found hidden in the workings of our Constitution, the notion that getting an abortion is a Constitutional right. Some estimate that sixty-million abortions were performed after *Roe.*

Stone v. Graham, 449 U.S. 39 (1980) struck down a Kentucky law requiring the posting of the Ten Commandments in public schools. Similar attacks on the public display of the Ten Commandments can be found in other court cases.

Lawrence v. Texas, 539 U.S. 558 (2003) overturned the 1986 U.S. Supreme Court decision in *Bowers v. Hardwick,* 478 U.S. 186, which upheld a Georgia statute outlawing sodomy.

U.S. v. Windsor, 570 U.S. 744 (2013) ruled that a portion of the 1996 Federal Defense of Marriage Act disallowing federal benefits to same-sex married couples is unconstitutional.

Obergefell v. Hodges, 576 U.S. 644 (2015) guaranteed the right to marry to same-sex couples.

You need not settle on my characterizations of *Roe*. In 2022 this 50-year-old travesty was overturned by the U.S. Supreme Court in *Dobbs v. Jackson Women's Health Organization, 142 S.Ct. 2228. Dobbs* confirms my initial reaction:

The Constitution makes no reference to abortion, and no such right is implicitly protected by any constitutional provision, including the one which the defenders of Roe and Casey now chiefly rely—the Due Process Clause of the Fourteenth Amendment. . . . An erroneous interpretation of the Constitution is always important, but some are more damaging than others. . . . Roe was also egregiously wrong and deeply damaging. For reasons already explained, Roe's constitutional analysis was far outside the bounds of any reasonable interpretation of the various constitutional provisions to which it vaguely pointed. Roe was on a collision course with the Constitution from the day it was decided. Casey perpetuated its errors, and those errors do not concern some arcane corner of the law of little importance to the American people. Rather, wielding nothing but 'raw judicial power,' Roe, 410 U.S., at 222 (White, J., dissenting), the court usurped the power to address a question of profound moral and social importance that the Constitution unequivocally leaves to the people.

Whether *Dobbs* signifies a return of moral considerations to the Court's deliberations remains to be seen. *Dobbs* does not, as falsely claimed by the media, end the "right" to get an abortion (which never existed in the Constitution in the first place.) It merely returns the decision to legalize or limit abortion to each state. Many states have already legalized it.

The "News" Media

Americans once trusted their news media to present truthful coverage. Most news outlets have become echo chambers for the socialist agenda, rejecting the truth in favor of slanted and inaccurate narratives and even outright lies. While Communist countries simply force their state-controlled media to parrot the party line, in a "free" country, it is equally effective if those who own and control the media subscribe to that agenda and willingly promote it. Our watchdog media that once kept our government in check has become a lap dog.

Biased news coverage was common well before I became aware of it. While compiling a book of veterans' memoirs, I spoke with Vietnam War veterans personally familiar with a battle known as the Tet Offensive. In 1968, the Communist-backed forces in North Vietnam mounted a massive attack during the Tet lunar holiday, when hostilities would typically abate for both sides. Our media, including one grandfatherly-appearing TV news anchor whom someone had christened "The Most Trusted Man in America," claimed that the attack had been a resounding defeat for American and South Vietnamese forces. This narrative exacerbated the volatile opposition to that war in America.

The veterans who knew better advised me that the opposite was true. Despite the surprise nature of the attack, American forces significantly prevailed. In retrospect, it is apparent that the media fanned the flames of the bitter divide, social upheaval, and riots spawned by that war. I was among those who had misplaced trust in our media at that time to report truthfully. Is the media repeating the same strategy today, stoking the divisions among us?

The news media's tactics, as well as its bias, warrant attention. Be aware of "the narrative," the orchestration of sound bites and phrases offered in the guise of news coverage that echo the official line across the entire spectrum of media outlets and talking heads so that no matter what station or source one listens to, the same words are heard. The tactic capitalizes on the psychological principle that when people hear the same thing repeatedly from multiple sources, even a lie will eventually settle in one's mind as being true.

Muzzling opposing voices is a long-standing tactic. Witness the recent firing and silencing of conservative voices and those who shine the spotlight on the misinformation spread concerning the Covid pandemic and the accompanying fear-mongering, including doctors and nurses who have lost their livelihoods for speaking the truth. When ideology is so weak and corrupt that it can't bear the smallest scrutiny or stand up to the truth, the last refuge is to silence or personally attack its opponents.

Accurate sources of information are difficult to locate as the movement to silence the truth gains momentum. In addition to seeking truthful sources, we must also develop a keen sense of discernment to distinguish the truth from lies. In the end, right will triumph, and wrong will meet its due.

The New World Order/One World Government

"Power tends to corrupt; absolute power corrupts absolutely." This oft-quoted phrase is attributed to John Dalberg Acton (Lord Acton), a late nineteenth- early- twentieth-century British historian. It recognizes that one's sense of morality lessens as one's power increases. Has the lust for wealth and power ever produced anything other than eventual destruction?

> Matthew 19:23-24: *Then Jesus said to his disciples, "Truly I tell you, it is hard for someone who is rich to enter the kingdom of heaven. Again I tell you, it is easier for a camel to go through the eye of a needle than for someone who is rich to enter the kingdom of God."*

History is littered with the ghosts of empires and people who sought to rule the world. Can Babylon or Assyria be found on a current map? Nearly a century ago, Nazi German dictator Adolph Hitler ignited WWII with his fantasy that his military conquests would enable pure Aryan Germans, the "master race," to rule the world. That war did not end well for him, the Nazis, or their allies.

Amidst our current turmoil, the phrase the "Great Reset" is being trumpeted by a collection of self-anointed elites who think engineering America's downfall will pave the way for the latest run at a new world order, setting their superior selves up to rule over the billions of their inferiors who inhabit the earth. Frequently lurking in these scenarios is a rumored shadowy, secret society of wealthy, powerful elites known as the Illuminati, who supposedly control world events behind the scenes.

God's counsel has much to teach us about this topic. The Book of Ecclesiastes, dated by scholars to about the tenth century B.C., offers some of the most pointed observations. Its authorship is generally attributed to Israel's King Solomon, one of the wealthiest and wisest men to have ever lived. (Some scholars attribute Ecclesiastes to other authors. Regardless of who penned its words, they provide sound guidance and wisdom.)

> Ecclesiastes 1:9, 11: *What has been will be again, what has been done will be done again; there is nothing new under the sun. . . . No one remembers the former generations, and even those yet to come will not be remembered by those who follow them.*
>
> Psalm 2:1-4: *Why do the nations conspire and the peoples plot in vain? The kings of the earth rise up and the rulers band together against the Lord and against his anointed, saying, "Let us break their chains and throw off their shackles." The One enthroned in heaven laughs; the Lord scoffs at them.*
>
> Matthew 16:26: *What good will it be for someone to gain the whole world, yet forfeit their soul? Or what can anyone gain in exchange for their soul?*
>
> Matthew 4:8-10: *Again, the devil took him [Jesus] to a very high mountain and showed him all the kingdoms of the world and their splendor. "All this I will give*

you," he said, "if you will bow down and worship me." Jesus said to him, "Away from me, Satan! For it is written: 'Worship the Lord your God, and serve him only.' "

1 Timothy 6:9-10: *Those who want to get rich fall into temptation and a trap into many foolish and harmful desires that plunge people into ruin and destruction. For the love of money is a root of all kinds of evil. Some people, eager for money, have wandered from the faith and pierced themselves with many griefs.*

Ecclesiastes 5:10: *Whoever loves money never has enough; whoever loves wealth is never satisfied with their income. This too is meaningless.*

Ecclesiastes 2:1-10 (excerpts): *I said to myself, "Come now, I will test you with pleasure to find out what is good." But that also proved to be meaningless. . . . what does pleasure accomplish? I tried cheering myself with wine, and embracing folly . . . I undertook great projects . . . houses for myself . . . planted vineyards . . . I made gardens and parks . . . I made reservoirs to water groves of flourishing trees . . . I bought male and female slaves . . . I also owned more herds and flocks than anyone in Jerusalem before me. I amassed silver and gold, and the treasure of kings and provinces. I acquired male and female singers, and a harem as well—the delights of a man's heart. I became greater by far than anyone in Jerusalem before me. . . . I denied myself nothing my eyes desired; . . . Yet when I surveyed all that my hands had done, and all what I toiled to achieve, everything was meaningless, a chasing after the wind; nothing was gained under the sun.*

Matthew 6:24: *No one can serve two masters. Either you will hate the one and love the other, or you will be devoted to the one and despise the other. You cannot serve both God and money.*

Ecclesiastes 12:13-14 (Solomon's parting summary): *Now all has been heard; here is the conclusion of the matter: Fear God and keep his commandments, for this is the duty of all mankind. For God will bring every deed into judgment, including every hidden thing, whether it is good or evil.*

Human attempts to create a one-world government have come and gone. But the Bible tells us that two such governments will appear in the future in connection with Jesus' return to Earth (see John 14:1-3; Luke 21:25-27; Matthew 24:30-31) not by man's hand but as and when ordained by God. While the Bible makes it clear that no one except God knows the day and time when Jesus will return, we are given signs that will precede His coming, and we are warned to be vigilant and ready for that return.

> 2 Timothy 3:1-5: *But mark this: There will be terrible times in the last days. People will be lovers of themselves, lovers of money, boastful, proud, abusive, disobedient to their parents, ungrateful, unholy, without love, unforgiving,*

> *slanderous, without self-control, brutal, not lovers of the good, treacherous, rash, conceited, lovers of pleasure rather than lovers of God—having a form of godliness but denying its power. Have nothing to do with such people.*
>
> Matthew 24:6-8: *You will hear of wars and rumors of wars, but see to it that you are not alarmed. Such things must happen, but the end is still to come. Nation will rise against nation, and kingdom against kingdom. There will be famines and earthquakes in various places. All these are the beginning of birth pains.*

Does our present level of social decay signal that we are near the end? Perhaps we are. But there have been prior periods when people thought that. *The Late, Great Planet Earth*, © 1970 by theologian Hal Lindsey, written shortly after the 1967 war in which Israel regained control of Jerusalem, concluded that we were on the verge of Jesus' return. Yet we continue to await that event over fifty years later, awash in turmoil and upheaval.

Cross Roads

The End Time Rulers

The first world ruler will be the "antichrist." Excerpts from 2 Corinthians 2-4 and 9-12 describe his advent:

> *... the day of the Lord ... will not come until the rebellion occurs and the man of lawlessness is revealed, the man doomed to destruction. He will oppose and will exalt himself over everything that is called God or is worshipped, so that he sets himself up in God's temple, proclaiming himself to be God. ... The coming of the lawless one will be in accordance with how Satan works. He will use all sorts of displays of power through signs and wonders that serve the lie, and all the ways that wickedness deceive those who are perishing. They perish because they refused to love the truth and so be saved. For this reason God sends them a powerful delusion so that they will believe the lie and so that all will be condemned who have not believed the truth but have delighted in wickedness.*

Revelation depicts this individual as a "beast" that will have total control of commerce. Revelation 13:16-17:

> *It also forced all people, great and small, rich and poor, free and slave, to receive a mark on their right hands or on their foreheads, so that they could not buy or sell unless they had the mark, which is the name of the beast or the number of its name.*

The beast will rule the entire world for a time until it/he is defeated and subdued by Jesus. Revelation 13:7-8:

> *It was given power to wage war against God's holy people, and to conquer them. And it was given authority over every tribe, people, language and nation. All inhabitants of the earth will worship the beast—all whose names have not been written in the Lamb's book of life, the Lamb who was slain from the creation of the world (*Jesus.*)*

Revelation 19 and 20 describe the defeat and binding of the beast. Revelation 19:20-21 and Revelation 20:1-2:

> *But the beast was captured, and with it the false prophet who had performed the signs on its behalf. With these signs he had deluded those who had received the mark of the beast and worshipped its image. The two of them were thrown alive into the fiery lake of burning sulfur. . . . And I saw an angel coming down out of heaven, having the key to the Abyss and holding in his hand a great chain. He seized the dragon, that ancient serpent, who is the devil or Satan, and bound him for a thousand years.*

After Satan is bound, Jesus will reign on Earth for a thousand years (Revelation 20.)

We spend a great deal of time fretting over whether America is about to fall, whether the end times are upon us, and which political candidates will gain office. No matter who comes to power, they will be imperfect, as are all humans, and they will fall short and disappoint us. Some will even work against us. Better to focus on the fact that God is in control and understand that no matter what happens on Earth, those who acknowledge Jesus as their Lord and Savior can find peace in their hope of Heaven.

Current observers suggest two important points of focus. First, we must keep our eyes upon Jerusalem, Israel, and the Middle East, as these are the epicenters where end-time events will unfold. Second, the recent movement to replace all forms of money with a global digital currency, and the current U.S. bank crisis that seem to have appeared without any precipitating causes other than as might be engineered by those seeking world domination, may be precursors to the antichrist mechanism of universal control over who can buy or sell. Constant vigilance is called for, as well as steadfast faith.

Cross Roads

God's Counsel for Mankind

So many instructions and warnings for every facet of our daily lives bombard us that we eventually tune them out, including those that may be important. Cars come with owner's manuals prepared by their makers that tell us when to service them and how to safely operate them. Red lights appear on the dashboard, and annoying chimes and beeps sound, even when a situation is so obvious that a two-year-old would notice it. Medicines bear dosage limits. When we ignore any of the maker's instructions and warnings or intentionally go counter to them, sometimes nothing bad happens, but other times really bad things can happen. It is important to figure out which instructions and warnings are life and death issues. Is the Bible an instruction and warning manual for life and death prepared for us by our Maker that we should not tune out?

Proverbs 14:12: *There is a way that appears to be right, but in the end it leads to death.*

Proverbs 12:15: *The way of fools seems right to them, but the wise listen to advice.*

Compare God's counsel on some of our most contentious issues to the directions we are taking. It matters not whether we are analyzing laws, political agendas, attempts to force acceptance of some lifestyle, practice, or social doctrine, our individual choices and behaviors, or any other aspect of our lives. God's standards remain the same.

Consider the consequences for us or our country if we continue down our present paths.

Cross Roads

Race Relations

> Galatians 3:28: *There is neither Jew nor Gentile, neither slave nor free, nor is there male and female, for you are all one in Christ Jesus.*

> Romans 3:10 (Amplified Bible): *As it is written, and forever remains written, "there is none righteous [none that meets God's standard], not even one."*

> Romans 3:23: *. . . for all have sinned and fall short of the glory of God.*

> Mark 12:31: *. . . Love your neighbor as yourself.*

> Matthew 5:44: *But I tell you, love your enemies and pray for those who persecute you.*

We are all one in God's eyes. What would our world look like if everyone lived by these principles? While many strive to bring us together, sadly, some promote discord and hatred. The Bible has no kind words for those who divide us:

> Proverbs 6:12-14: *A troublemaker and a villain, who goes about with a corrupt mouth, . . . who plots evil in his heart—he always stirs up conflict.*

> Proverbs 6:16-19: *There are six things the Lord hates, . . . a person who stirs up conflict in the community*

> Proverbs 10:12: *Hatred stirs up conflict, but love covers all wrongs.*

Proverbs 16:28: *A perverse person stirs up conflict, and a gossip separates close friends.*

Proverbs 29:22: *An angry person stirs up conflict, and a hot-tempered person commits many sins.*

Love or hate? Our choice.

Gender and Marriage

Genesis 1:27: *So God created mankind in his own image, in the image of God he created them; male and female he created them.*

Genesis 5:1-2: *This is the written account of Adam's family line. When God created mankind, he made them in the likeness of God. He created them male and female and he blessed them. And he named them "Mankind" when they were created*

Genesis 2:20-24: *But for Adam, no suitable helper was found. So the Lord God caused the man to fall into a deep sleep; and while he was sleeping, he took one of the man's ribs and then closed up the place with flesh. Then the Lord God made a woman from the rib he had taken out of the man, and he brought her to the man. The man said, "This is now bone of my bones and flesh of my flesh; she shall be called 'woman,' for she was taken out of a man." This is why a man leaves his father and mother and is united to his wife, and they become one flesh.*

1 Corinthians 7:10: *To the married I give this command (not I, but the Lord): A wife must not separate from her husband. But if she does, she must remain unmarried or else be reconciled to her husband. And a husband must not divorce his wife.*

Is marriage a relationship created and defined by God, or something that people invented and can redefine at will? What end is in store for those who advocate or choose defiance of the way God created us and who force this upon children? As you consider this issue, keep in mind that anyone who simply points out what God says about something is not trying to impose their views on someone else or deprive someone of their "rights." Attacking the messenger never alters God's word nor erases the consequences of our actions.

Deceitfulness

John 1:17: *For the law was given through Moses; grace and truth came through Jesus Christ.*

John 14:6: *Jesus answered, "I am the way, the truth and the life. No one comes to the Father except through me."*

John 8:31-32: *To the Jews who had believed him, Jesus said, "If you hold to my teaching, you are really my disciples. Then you will know the truth, and the truth will set you free."*

John 8:44: *You belong to your father, the devil, and you want to carry out your father's desires. He was a murderer from the beginning, not holding to the truth, for there is no truth in him. When he lies, he speaks his native language, for he is a liar and the father of lies.*

Proverbs 19:9: *A false witness will not go unpunished, and whoever pours out lies will perish.*

Proverbs 6:16-19: *There are six things the Lord hates, seven that are detestable to him: haughty eyes, a lying tongue, hands that shed innocent blood, a heart that devises wicked schemes, feet that are quick to rush into evil, a false witness who pours out lies, and a person who stirs up conflict in the community.*

Is the practice of habitual lying a wise way to live one's life?

Freeloading

2 Thessalonians 6-10: . . . keep away from every believer who is idle and disruptive . . . you yourselves know how you ought to follow our example. We were not idle when we were with you, nor did we eat anyone's food without paying for it. On the contrary, we worked night and day, laboring and toiling so that we would not be a burden to any of you. We did this not because we do not have the right to such help, but in order to offer ourselves as a model for you to imitate. For even when we were with you, we gave you this rule: "The one who is unwilling to work shall not eat."

The Value of Children; Abortion

Psalm 127:3: *Children are a heritage from the Lord, offspring a reward from him.*

Jeremiah 1:4-5: *The word of the Lord came to me, saying, "Before I formed you in the womb I knew you, before you were born I set you apart; . . ."*

Psalm 139:13-16: *For you created my innermost being; you knit me together in my mother's womb. I praise you because I am fearfully and wonderfully made; your works are wonderful, I know that full well. My frame was not hidden from you when I was made in the secret place, when I was woven together in the depths of the earth. Your eyes saw my unformed body; all the days ordained for me were written in your book before one of them came to be.*

Mark 10:14-16: *People were bringing little children to Jesus for him to place his hands on them, but the disciples rebuked them. When Jesus saw this, he was indignant. He said to them, "Let the little children come to me, and do not hinder them, for the kingdom of God belongs to such as these. Truly I tell you, anyone who will not receive the kingdom of God like a little child will never enter it." And he took the children in his arms, placed his hands on them and blessed them.*

Exodus 20:13: *You shall not murder.*

Those Who Harm Children or Cause Them to Sin or Lose Faith

> Mark 9:36: *He took a little child whom he placed among them. Taking the child in his arms, he said to them, "Whoever welcomes one of these little children in my name welcomes me;"* . . .

> Luke 17:1-2: *Jesus said to his disciples, "Things that cause people to stumble are bound to come, but woe to anyone through whom they come. It would be better for them to be thrown into the sea with a millstone tied around their neck than to cause one of these little ones to stumble."*

Morality

Exodus 20:14: *You shall not commit adultery.*

Exodus 20:17: *...You shall not covet your neighbor's wife.*

Ephesians 5:3-6: *But among you there must not be even a hint of sexual immorality, or of any kind of impurity, or of greed, because these are improper for God's people. Nor should there be any obscenity, foolish talk or coarse joking, which are out of place, but of thanksgiving. For of this you can be sure: No immoral, impure or greedy person—such a erson is an idolater—has any inheritance in the kingdom of Christ and God. Let no one deceive you with empty words, for because of such things God's wrath comes on those who are disobedient.*

Colossians 3:5-6: *Put to death, therefore, whatever belongs to your earthly nature: sexual immorality, impurity, lust, evil desires and greed. Because of these, the wrath of God is coming.*

Hebrews 13:4: *Marriage should be honored by all, and the marriage bed kept pure, for God will judge the adulterer and all the sexually immoral.*

1 Corinthians 6:9: *Or do you not know that wrongdoers will not inherit the kingdom of God? Do not be deceived: Neither the sexually immoral nor idolaters nor adulterers nor men who have sex with men nor thieves nor the greedy nor drunkards nor*

slanderers nor swindlers will inherit the kingdom of God.

Romans 1:24-26: *Therefore God gave them over in the sinful desires of their hearts to sexual impurity for the degrading of their bodies with one another. They exchanged the truth about God for a lie, and worshipped and served created things [*man-made idols*] rather than the Creator—who is forever praised. Amen. Because of this, God gave them over to shameful lusts. Even their women exchanged natural sexual relations for unnatural ones. In the same way the men also abandoned natural relations with women and were inflamed with lust for one another. Men committed shameful acts with other men, and received in themselves the due penalty for their error.*

The Invisible Battle for America

Confronting the Unseen

Our Western mindset tends to dismiss the notion of a spirit realm. We focus on the visible, tangible, audible world in which we live, where science can explain everything. Yet we experience invisible things every day, such as wind, germs, and odors. The Bible, however, is clear that there is another dimension in which the battle between good and evil is waged that profoundly affects our lives.

God himself is Spirit (John 4:24.) He has existed eternally in the realm we call Heaven and dwells there with angels, beings He created who do His bidding (Psalm 8:5.) Long ago, a fallen angel known as Satan (the devil) rebelled against God and was cast out of Heaven together with his followers (demons.) They have sought to corrupt and separate mankind from God since the dawn of creation.

God will banish them . . . *into the eternal fire prepared for the devil and his angels* (Matthew 25:41) in the end times when Jesus returns to earth. Until this happens, they will continue to wield considerable influence over mankind.

> Ephesians 6:12: *For our struggle is not against flesh and blood, but against the rulers, against the authorities, against the powers of this dark world, and against the spiritual forces of evil in the heavenly realms.*

Our minds are the primary battlefields. Everything we do or say, even the thoughts that constantly occupy our minds, are triggered by a thought. It is said that it is impossible to empty our minds of all thoughts; there is always something there. This is an interesting concept to test if you are so inclined.

In fighting this conflict, we need to remain aware of where our thoughts come from and how they measure against the truth taught by the Bible. 1 Corinthians 10:5: . . . *take captive every thought to make it obedient to Christ.* In other words, think about what you're thinking about.

The enemy can promote lies through what others say, but also as thoughts. Satan's lies, . . . *the flaming arrows of the evil one* (Ephesians 6:16) such as, "God could never forgive you for what you have done," can lodge in our minds as true unless we learn to recognize them as lies and reject them.

> Ephesians 2:1-2: *As for you [the Christians in Ephesus], you were dead in your transgressions and sins, in which you used to live when you followed the ways of this world and of the ruler of the kingdom of the air, the spirit who is now at work in those who are disobedient.*
>
> The Zondervan Study Bible's marginal comment notes: *The ruler described here is Satan. The term air was used in the ancient world to refer to the spiritual realms where demons operated in the lives of people who refused God's authority.*

> John 8:44: *. . . He [Satan] was a murderer from the beginning, not holding to the truth, for there is no truth in him. When he lies, he speaks his native language, for he is a liar and the father of lies.*
>
> 2 Corinthians 11:14: *. . . Satan himself masquerades as an angel of light.*
>
> 1 Peter 5:8: *. . . Your enemy the devil prowls around like a roaring lion looking for someone to devour.*
>
> 1 John 5:18-19 (New Living Translation): *We know that God's children do not make a practice of sinning. We know that we are children of God and that the world around us is under the control of the evil one.*

In addition to the mental battle, the Bible describes people who were physically possessed by demons, e.g.:

> Luke 4:33-35: *In the synagogue there was a man possessed by a demon, an impure spirit. He [the demon] cried out at the top of his voice, "Go away! What do you want with us, Jesus of Nazareth? Have you come to destroy us? I know who you are—the Holy One of God!" "Be quiet!" Jesus said sternly. "Come out of him!" then the demon threw the man down before them all and came out without injuring him.* (See also Matthew 4:24, 8:16, 8:28, 8:33, and 12:22).

Can people still become inhabited by demons (or controlled by evil spirits?) Adolph Hitler, for example, mesmerized an entire country with his fiery rhetoric and was responsible for the genocide of six million Jews during WWII.

The Bible warns that we should never engage with the occult forces that inhabit the dark realms.

> *Let no one be found among you who sacrifices their son or daughter in the fire, who practices divination or sorcery, interprets omens, engages in witchcraft, or casts spells, or who is a medium or spiritist or who consults the dead. Anyone who does these things is detestable to the Lord* (Deuteronomy 18:10-12.)

Israel's Apostasy

Severe judgments befell ancient Israel when the people turned away from God and began worshipping man-made idols and multiple pagan gods. Has the same fate befallen America?

Judges 2:10-15 recapitulates the consequences of one of Israel's falls into apostasy:

> *After that whole generation [of Joshua's contemporaries] had been gathered to their ancestors, another generation grew up who neither knew the Lord nor what he had done for Israel. Then the Israelites did evil in the eyes of the Lord and served the Baals. They forsook the Lord, the God of their ancestors, who had brought them out of Egypt. They followed and worshipped various gods of the people around them. They aroused the Lord's anger because they forsook him and served Baal and the Ashtoreths [descriptions of Baal and Ashtoreth follow]. In his anger against Israel the Lord gave them into the hands of raiders who plundered them. He sold them into the hands of their enemies all around, whom they were no longer able to resist. Whenever Israel went out to fight, the hand of the Lord was against them to defeat them, just as he had sworn to them. They were in great distress.*

How close is this description to America's journey since the Pilgrims landed?

Cross Roads

When God is Expelled, What Steps In?

Messianic Rabbi and author Jonathan Cahn offers a credible explanation of the depths to which America has now fallen in his book, *The Return of the Gods*. He concludes that the series of Supreme Court decisions outlined above are the chief catalysts in America's accelerating downfall. His premise is consistent with the rapid pace of America's decay that began in the 1960s. The spiritual void created by our apostasy has been filled by the gods that once ruled the ancient world. The process is described in Luke 11:24-26:

> *When an impure spirit comes out of a person, it goes through arid places seeking rest and does not find it. Then it says, I will return to the house I left." When it arrives, it finds the house swept clean and put in order. Then it goes and takes seven other spirits more wicked than itself, and they go in and live there. And the final condition of that person is worse than the first.*

The marginal comment in the Zondervan *NIV Study Bible* adds:

On one level, this was a metaphor for Israel (Mt 12:45): the Messiah had come to redeem the nation, but most rejected the opportunity, which left them vulnerable to increased demonic influence. But there is another lesson: When a demon is removed, the "vacuum" left behind must be filled with the Holy Spirit. If it is not, the demon will return with additional demons. The same is true of sinful behaviors. The person's condition is worse than it was before.

Accepting the reality of an invisible realm populated by malevolent spirit beings that have existed for thousands of years or more and are capable of negatively influencing human thoughts and behaviors can be challenging. Neither denial nor scoffing will counter it. Defense is mandated.

The presence of God's Spirit is powerful enough to drive demons away. But when God is cast aside, foul spirits enter the vacant space and afflict evil behavior.

Israel's episodes of idol worship were more than just bowing down to man-made objects. They were, at their core, demon worship. 1 Corinthians 10:20 (Amplified Bible):

> *On the contrary, the things which the Gentiles (pagans) sacrifice, they sacrifice to demons [in effect], and not to God; and I do not want you to become partners with demons [by eating at feasts in pagan temples].*

Ezekiel 23:37-40 goes deeper:

> *For they have committed adultery and blood is on their hands. They committed adultery with their idols, they even sacrificed their children, whom they bore to me, as food for them. They have also done this to me: At that same time they defiled my sanctuary and desecrated my Sabbath. On the very day they sacrificed their children to their idols, they entered my sanctuary and desecrated it. This is what they did in my house.*

Cahn identifies three principal gods (evil spirits affiliated with Satan) that occupy different spheres of control. Baal orchestrates a nation's turning away from God. Ishtar (known in the Bible as Ashtoreth) then ushers in sexual immorality. Molech is associated with the child sacrifices abhorrent to God. Israel's worship of Baal and Ashtoreth is specifically condemned in Judges 2:10-15, quoted above.

The gods were, and are, kept at bay through God's presence and power. They were marginalized in ancient Israel when it was obedient to God. Their influence was blunted in some parts of the Middle East and surrounding territories with the advent of Christianity 2,000 years ago. America's founding and openly acknowledged and practiced Biblical principles that persisted into the late-19th and early-20th centuries minimized their influence. Cahn suggests that, in the same manner as these gods ruled the ancient world and returned to dominate Israel in its cycles of apostasy, so have they now come to roost in America.

Baal's success in America is evident. For some years, God was gradually nudged aside. Since the 1960s, He and His Word have been methodically and forcefully banished. The path is now paved for outright persecution of Christians. It has been occurring for years in other parts of the world. Do we assume it cannot happen here? Are we experiencing its early stages?

Baal's removal of God and the Bible sets the stage for Ishtar. She is the goddess of all things sexual, down to the basest levels of prostitution, every form of deviancy and perversion, mutilation, gender changing, free love, destruction of marriage and reversal of natural gender roles, and drunken or drug-induced orgies. Ishtar, or an iteration, also doubles as the goddess of love, war, and destruction. Long ago, she assumed a benign presence in our culture as the goddess of love we call Venus or Aphrodite. Cahn notes that America's growing acceptance of homosexuality and abortion since the 1960s, spiraling downward to today's advocations of mutilating operations and gender multiplication, are hallmarks of Ishtar's campaign to progressively obliterate God's Word and ruin His creation.

Molech, associated with the pagan rites of child sacrifice, is seen as duplicating that influence by encouraging the acceptance of abortion, progressing to the current persecution of those who oppose it. Cahn is rightly dismayed at America's role in exporting abortion to other countries. Has America equaled or exceeded Molech's ancient accomplishments?

Tracing America's downfall beginning in the 1960s is not difficult. The "Summer of Love" promoting the sexual revolution (dubbed the "new morality" but merely a re-emergence of pagan promiscuity); acceptance and proliferation of drug usage; acceleration of the divorce rate, pre- and extramarital sex; women's "liberation;" rising numbers of children born out of wedlock, to single-parent households, and unmarried cohabitation; declining church attendance; substitution of "if it feels good, do it" for prevailing moral limits; court decisions removing our founding faith from public schools and the public sphere—the list could go on.

It is chilling to confront the existence of an invisible realm inhabited by malevolent spirits who wish to harm mankind and even more so to consider the depths of evil they exert. Retreating into the psychological defense of denial will only allow things to become worse. We are called to confront this and have been given the power and weapons to win.

Until recently, America has been spared from the moral collapse and unspeakable evils that have plagued other times and places, such as the persecution and slaughter of Christians in the Middle East and the genocides that have swept through Europe and Eurasia. The levels emerging in contemporary America are unexpected. We seem unprepared and even unwilling to counter them. Our pulpits largely remain silent in the face of this onslaught. Author Eric Metaxas has suggested that the silence from our pulpits is comparable to the failure of Germany's churches to speak out against the rise of Nazi Germany (*Letter to the American Churches*, © Eric Metaxas, 2022, Salem Books, Washington, D.C.) But we should be cautious about dissension within the church during times when it is essential to remain united. When the church is fractured, the enemy gains ground.

Despite our dark hours, those who believe in Jesus are blessed with the hope and promise of eternal salvation. God and His righteousness will prevail no matter how bad things might appear.

Cross Roads

Our Invincible Hope

Winning the Battle

Those who say "Yes" to Jesus are secure in that relationship for eternity. The devil has no claim on them, nor does death. Romans 8:38-39:

> *For I am convinced that neither death nor life, neither angels nor demons, neither the present nor the future, nor any powers neither height nor depth, nor anything else in all creation, will be able to separate us from the love of God that is in Christ Jesus.*

However, during the remainder of our mortal lives, we will continually struggle to overcome the temptations of our sinful natures, as well as the lies the enemy plants in our minds. Knowing God's truth to defeat the enemy's lies requires studying and knowing what the Bible says. But there is more. We are equipped to fight this battle and told how to do so. Ephesians 6:10-18:

> *Finally, be strong in the Lord and in his mighty power. Put on the full armor of God, so that you can take your stand against the devil's schemes. For our struggle is not against flesh and blood, but against the rulers, against the authorities, against the powers of this dark world and against the spiritual forces of evil in the heavenly realms. Therefore, put on the full armor of God so that when the day of evil comes, you may be able to stand your ground, and after you have done*

everything, to stand. Stand firm then, with the belt of truth buckled around your waist, with the breastplate of righteousness in place, and with your feet fitted with the readiness that comes from the gospel of peace. In addition to all this, take up the shield of faith, with which you can extinguish all the flaming arrows of the evil one. Take the helmet of salvation and the sword of the Spirit, which is the word of God. And pray in the Spirit on all occasions, with all kinds of prayers and requests. With this in mind, be alert and always keep on praying for all the Lord's people.

Be not discouraged nor plagued with doubt or fear. The Bible teaches that we will all experience trials and tribulations throughout life. Persevere and gain strength through prayer and faith in God's promises. If you have become one of God's children by faith in Jesus, you will prevail.

Revival or Collapse?

God gave Israel's King Solomon the path towards the healing of a nation in 2 Chronicles 7:13-14:

> *"When I shut up the heavens so that there is no rain, or command locusts to devour the land or send a plague among my people, if my people, who are called by my name, will humble themselves and pray and seek my face and turn from their wicked ways, then I will hear from heaven, and I will forgive their sin and will heal their land.*

America has experienced ten or more major revivals beginning in 1734. A well-researched summary of those written by Patrick Morley, dated October 12, 2022, can be found at churchleaders.com/outreach-missions-articles/257668. Some readers will be familiar with recent revivals and those who led them.

1. From 1947-1950, well-known evangelists Bill Bright (the founder of Campus Crusade for Christ, now known as Cru) and Billy Graham led many thousands to the Lord. The Christian Businessmen's Committee (CBMC) was founded in this period. In 1950, a revival at Wheaton College spread to other campuses. Campus Crusade developed *The Jesus Film* and began distributing it in the early 1980s (now a separate ministry) as an outreach to non-English speaking countries with little or no exposure to the gospel. It depicts the life of Jesus based on Luke's gospel. It has been translated into more than 2,000 languages,

reaching into the darkest nations where Christianity is persecuted and other corners of the globe where people are experiencing the gospel in their language for the very first time. Its viewership is measured in multiple millions.

2. The late 1960s and early 1970s witnessed several awakenings. The "I Found It" campaign flourished with billboards and bumper stickers. A college campus revival in 1970 at Asbury College in Wilmore, KY, spread to other campuses. Pastor Chuck Smith of Calvary Chapel in California opened his church doors to the marginalized "hippie" community. Pastor Smith's open heart brought countless young people to the Lord. The Jesus Movement was the larger manifestation of this beginning. The Pentecostal community was active in revival campaigns. (The Charismatic and Pentecostal Movements are originally attributed to William Seymour, a black pastor who was blind in one eye, in 1909. This coincided with a movement started by Billy Sunday in 1905 that saw an estimated one million people come to faith.)

3. From 1991-2000, the Promise Keepers movement that was started by former Colorado University football coach Bill McCartney in 1990 saw an estimated five million men attend its gatherings. It succeeded in crossing racial barriers and encouraging countless men to become spiritual leaders in their families and communities.

The Supreme Court decision in 2022 overturning *Roe v. Wade* could be a step towards turning America in the right direction. There are recent sparks of awakening and repentance, such as the 2023 revival gathering at Asbury College, mirroring the 1970 revival that started there. A newly-released movie entitled *The Jesus Movement* recounts Chuck Smith's revival in 1971. The discussions prompted by that movie reveal a surprising number of people who were brought to faith through his outreach.

It cannot be known what might be required of America to merit God's healing. *Roe* was unjustifiable as a legal decision from the start. But the other decisions listed would be harder to overturn as they might survive legal scrutiny, leaving their wrongful natures based on affronts to God's standards in the Bible. The old quip, "You can't legislate morality," comes to mind. Perhaps a wholesale house cleaning from local school boards to Congress and the White House will be needed to reverse our situation. Does America have enough people who seek righteousness to accomplish this?

While we may feel that individually we can do little to reverse what is happening, we can pray for our country to awaken and return to God. The power of prayer can accomplish great things.

Cross Roads

Is Your Eternal Destiny Secure?

Individually, we have had the means to escape the final judgment awaiting the forces of evil for over two thousand years by accepting God's gift of salvation through faith in Jesus Christ.

> *If you declare with your mouth, "Jesus is Lord," and believe in your heart that God raised him from the dead, you will be saved.* Romans 10:9.

If you have considered saying "Yes" to Jesus but have not taken that step or are unsure of how to do so, a simple prayer from your heart, something like the following, is all that is needed. God knows your heart and will understand your prayer.

> Dear Lord Jesus, I know that I am a sinner, and I ask for your forgiveness. I believe you died for my sins and rose from the dead. I turn from my sins and invite you to come into my life. I want to trust and follow you as my Lord and Savior.

None of us can truly know when our own lives will end. Accidents, illness, and other mishaps can suddenly cut short our lives before we live out our expected life span of 70 to 80 years. Our time to say "Yes" is finite and uncertain.

The Bible tells us there are only two possible eternal destinations for everyone after our mortal lives end. One is Heaven, the incomparably-beautiful home with God for all who have said "Yes" to Jesus, whose names will be written in the Book of Life. There will be no more tears, crying, or pain there. The hope of Heaven is a powerful antidote to the chaos in which we live, knowing that our suffering is finite.

The other eternal destination is described in Revelation 20:15: *Anyone whose name was not found written in the Book of Life was thrown into the lake of fire.* This is a place of pain and anguish that will never end. Is there any good reason to say "No" to Jesus or to delay this decision?

> John 3:16: *For God so loved the world that he gave his one and only Son, that whoever believes in him shall not perish but have eternal life.*

Epilogue

Luke 11:17: *Every kingdom divided against itself is doomed to destruction; and a house divided against itself falls.* America retained a cohesive moral structure based on widely shared Biblical principles for about three hundred years after the Massachusetts Pilgrims landed. There were certainly some who were not of a like mind, but for the most part, the country realized the need for God's hand in its affairs. The teaching in our schools, and our public discourse, reflected this.

In the 1800s, doctrines emerged that created growing rifts in the social fabric. As the twentieth century blossomed, more and more people enjoyed prosperity and success, transitioning from agriculture to urban living and jobs. Electric- and gasoline-powered devices, flying machines, moving pictures, radio, and television expanded our horizons to encompass the entire world. Medical technology and discoveries conquered dreaded diseases. Life spans increased. And all of these new wonders were created through mankind's ingenuity and science! However, another reality awaited its chance to enter the picture.

Since time began, God's kingdom and His people have faced a potent invisible adversary unhindered by humanity's mortal life span, intent on tearing down God's kingdom, separating His people from Him, and ultimately replacing God with other objects of worship. The adversary is aided by people who share his goals, perhaps thinking that by doing so, they can gain wealth and power. If the adversary prevails, God is completely removed from a nation. The void created is filled with malevolent spirits that destroy a nation from within, as well as its citizens. Is this America in 2023? If so, how do we respond, collectively and individually?

Individually we have the free will to accept God's gift of eternal life by placing our trust and faith in Jesus Christ as our Lord and Savior. This cannot be taken from us, though we will face trials and tribulations during our life on Earth. People in other parts of the world have been persecuted for many years because of their faith, yet they refuse to renounce it. Will Americans have the same resolve if it comes to that here?

The fate of our nation is another matter. God has provided the way for a nation to repent and return to Him. Whether America is able or willing to do that remains to be seen. On another level, if we are approaching the final days when Jesus will return, then events will unfold as they are depicted in prophecy.

Ultimately, since our eternal destinies are at stake, it won't matter much who is sitting in the White House or what is going on in the world around us when we take our final breath. The Bible says we should work out our salvation with fear and trembling. We only need to make the right choice.

About the Author

James Downey earned a B.S. degree in Psychology and a Juris Doctor degree in Law from the University of Nebraska. After serving a term in the U.S. Army, he practiced law for thirty years, retiring in 2004. In the 1980s, he began a comparative religion study, exploring Buddhism, Hinduism, Taoism, New Age, Catholicism, Islam, Judaism, Mormonism, and the principal Protestant denominations. He has attended and taught in denominational and nondenominational churches in four states, also serving as an elder and deacon. Travels through Israel, Jordan, Egypt, and The Vatican added first-hand exposure to their predominant religious practices.

His first book, *The Evolution of Jihad* (written under the pen name of H. Davidson,) explores the roots of Islam and how the search for the one true God of Abraham evolved into today's terrorism. *Why?* and *Dying to Live* speak to the questions of why a loving God permits the destructive chaos enveloping the world and what happens to us after we take our final breath. In a shift of direction, *Brothers in Arms* recounts memoirs and life stories of veterans, victims, heroes, and survivors of WWII, The Korean War, and the Vietnam War. Their stories are accompanied by 130 historical documents and photographs, many from their private collections. The author's books are available on Amazon.

The author can be contacted at: j.d.vrod@gmail.com.

Bibliography and Further Resources

The Return of the Gods, © 2022 by Jonathan Cahn, Published by FrontLine, an Imprint of Charisma Media, 600 Rinehart Road, Lake Mary, Florida 32746.

The End Times in Chronological Order, © 2012 by Ron Rhodes, Published by Harvest House Publishers, Eugene, Oregon 97408.

The Father of Hollywood, © 2006 by Gaelyn Whitley Keith, BookSurge; www.booksurge.com.

The Christian History of the Constitution of the United States of America, © 1960, 1966, by Vera M. Hall, Published by The Foundation for American Christian Education, Box 27035, San Francisco, CA 94127, preface and other sections.

Teaching and Learning America's Christian History, © 1965 by Rosalie J. Slater, Published by The Foundation for American Christian Education, 2946 Twenty-Fifth Ave., San Francisco, CA.

The One Year Christian History by Sharon O. Rusten and E. Michael Rusten, Tyndale House Publishers, © 2003, pages 512-513.

Letter to the American Church, © 2022 by Eric Metaxas, Published by Salem Books, An Imprint of Regnery Publishing, A Division of Salem Media Group, Washington, D.C.

The Case for Faith, © 2000 by Lee Strobel, Zondervan, Grand Rapids, MI 49520.

Deadly Times, © 2015 By Lew Erwin, Globe Pequot Press.

Encyclopedia Britannica, online version; posting on Horace Mann by Lawrence A. Cremin; biography of Emma Hart Willard.

The First Amendment Encyclopedia, Middle Tennessee State University, "Horace Mann" by David Carleton; Scopes Monkey Trial by James C. Foster; www.mtsu.edu.

Principles of Liberty in our Founding Documents, and The Declaration of Independence, National Center for Constitutional Studies, online, Earl Taylor, Jr.

The General Society of Mayflower Descendants; The Mayflower Society; posting on the Pilgrims and *The Mayflower Compact*; themayflowersociety.org.

U.S. Library of Congress website: Horace Mann. Churchleaders.com/outreach-missins/outreach-missions/articles/257668-brief-history-spiritual-revival-awakening-america.html; Patrick Morley.

Cross Roads

Made in the USA
Monee, IL
11 January 2025

74856050R00066